Gluten-free Vegan:

Healthy Everyday Dishes in under 30 minutes

Contents

Disclaimer

October 2014 – Second edition. Gluten-free Vegan has been updated to include 40 FULL recipes and 20 photos to accompany them.

Introduction

Changing over to a new or a healthier diet is one such perennial resolution that most of us have probably made this year (well, most of us make this resolution every year really) and finds it really hard to stick to it.

It's true that keeping resolutions about healthy eating are more down to our ability to steer clear of the unhealthy foods that we see every day. This particular book was inspired by the latest plant based gluten-free diet that has all nutritional circles talking.

There are many reasons why you may have decided that being vegan and gluten-free is the diet for you. You might want to give up eating animals and animal based products because you're a fierce wildlife protector or you may be suffering from the bad side effects of gluten based foods. You could even just want to try it as a weight loss diet to see whether this particular diet can help you lose some pounds other diets have failed to help you with. The real dilemma with such diets is always, 'WHAT DO I EAT?!' or 'WHAT INGREDIENT'S DO I USE?'

If this is the case then this book will tell you exactly what to expect from a gluten-free vegan diet and how to use the diet approved ingredients to whip up healthy, easy and yummy meals that won't make you feel as though you are missing out on something.

Conversion Charts

I have included easy conversion charts so everyone can use this book, wherever in the world you are!

Cooking/ Baking Measurements

Volume Conversions		Weight Conversions		Temperature Conversion	
Imperial	**Metric**	**Oz**	**Grams**	**Celsius**	**Fahrenheit**
1 tsp	5 ml	½	15	120	225
1 tbsp	15 ml	1	30	150	300
¼ cup	60 ml	3	90	160	325
1/3 cup	75 ml	4	115	180	350
½ cup	125 ml	8	225	190	375
2/3 cup	150 ml	12	350	200	400
¾ cup	175 ml	1 pound	450	220	425
1 cup	250 ml	2 ¼ pounds	1 Kg	230	450

Note: All conversions are approximate and rounded to the nearest value.

Handy Conversions

3 tsp	=	1 tbsp	1 dash	=	6 drops	1 pound flour	=	3 ½ cups
4 tbsp	=	¼ cup	3 tsp	=	½ oz	1 pound sugar	=	2 ¼ cups
5tbsp + 1tsp	=	1/3 cup	48 tsp	=	1 cup	1 stick butter	=	¼ pound/110 gms
8 tbsp	=	½ cup	1 pint	=	16 oz/ 2 cups	1 pinch	=	Less than 1/8 tsp
10tbsp + 2 tsp	=	2/3 cup	1 Quart	=	2 pints/ 4 cups			
12 tbsp	=	¾ cup	1 Gallon	=	4 qt/ 16 cups			
16 tbsp	=	1 cup	1.2 tsp (US)	=	1 tsp (UK)			

Dry Weight Measurements

		Ounces	Pounds	Metric
1/16 teaspoon	a dash			
1/8 teaspoon or less	a pinch or 6 drops			.5 ml
1/4 teaspoon	15 drops			1 ml
1/2 teaspoon	30 drops			2 ml
1 teaspoon	1/3 tablespoon	1/6 ounce		5 ml
3 teaspoons	1 tablespoon	1/2 ounce		14 grams
1 tablespoon	3 teaspoons	1/2 ounce		14 grams
2 tablespoons	1/8 cup	1 ounce		28 grams
4 tablespoons	1/4 cup	2 ounces		56.7 grams
5 tablespoons plus 1 teaspoon	1/3 cup	2.6 ounces		75.6 grams
8 tablespoons	1/2 cup	4 ounces	1/4 pound	113.4 grams
10 tablespoons plus 2 teaspoons	2/3 cup	5.2 ounces		158 ml
12 tablespoons	3/4 cup	6 ounces	.375 pound	177 ml
16 tablespoons	1 cup	8 ounces	1/2 pound	225 ml
32 tablespoons	2 cups	16 ounces	1 pound	450 ml
64 tablespoons	4 cups or 1 quart	32 ounces	2 pounds	907 ml

What is gluten?

There are many products that are touted as gluten-free and vegan friendly but what does this mean? Gluten allergies are on the rise these days with the introduction of gluten in most foods. Gluten is a protein that is present in all wheat products and many processed foods which contain wheat and grains like barley and rye. Even lubricants, pills and cosmetics contain gluten. Gluten is what gives bread its bounce and elasticity. That's right, the fluffy, bouncy texture in cakes and breads is due to the presence of gluten!

Over the last ten years many people have been diagnosed allergic to gluten and products that contain gluten because it can harm their intestinal lining and cause serious health problems. There are several of us who experience unexplained bloating, fatigue and anaemia and there are many of us who remain undiagnosed of celiac disease to this day.

However, even if you're not gluten sensitive you may find it interesting to know that gluten in processed foods serves as empty calories. It's not the gluten that helps in increasing your weight but the processed foods that make you pack on the pounds and avoiding them will likely cause weight loss immediately (wheat gluten can be addictive)

What is vegan?

To those of us who confuse vegan with just being vegetarian - being a vegetarian means that you may exclude animal proteins mostly and may eat products that are derived from animals like milk and other dairy products. Being vegan means not eating any animal derived products or by products like dairy, eggs and even animal gelatin. Vegans have a more restricted diet than vegetarians and avoid animal products whether obtained through slaughtering or not.

The main concern for people who are thinking of converting to Veganism is whether they are missing out on important nutrients and vitamins that are found in meat and dairy products. Many vegan and gluten-free ingredients contain those vitamins in abundance and help you keep a healthy body and mind.

This book will introduce you to fresh and everyday recipes that you can use to start on your gluten-free vegan diet and enrich your body with all those important nutrients.

Ok let's get started!

Quick Fixes

Many of us are too tired after the day's work, handling kids and wrangling time between keeping a clean house and making time for yourself to be in the kitchen for a couple of hours. Wouldn't it be great if you could prepare a gluten-free vegan meal on the fly? In under 30 minutes to be exact. This is something that can be accomplished easily if you follow the tips below:

- Keep any leftover vegetable broth from a recipe and freeze it for use on a later day. Especially on days you don't have time to make more of it.
- Keep packs of beans and lentils, the dried variety, in your pantry or cook them in batches and store them in your freezer for those days when you feel exhausted and would like a quick fix meal. Canned tomatoes can be really versatile in their use so stock up your shelves with them.
- Keep flax seeds to make flax 'eggs' (egg substitute) for use in recipes where you might have used eggs before converting over to this diet. To make flax eggs you mix one tablespoons of ground flax seeds with one three tablespoons of water and leave to 'set'.
- Keep refrigerated staples like black and green olives, sundried tomatoes, tomato salsa, gluten-free vegan sauces, almond milk, coconut milk, nut butters and non-dairy cheese.
- Set aside a few hours of kitchen time for pre-prepping meals. On days you find free time it might be a good idea to prepare broth with those veggies that may go to waste if you don't use them immediately or boil the lentils and beans that you can freeze for later.
- Make your pizza and pie crusts, cover and freeze for those days you can just muster up enough energy to slap on toppings and give it a shove in the oven.
- Use your leftovers to create a nice medley and just make a quick side dish to go along with them.

- Buy gluten-free vegan pizza crusts, burgers and frozen pizzas from companies such as Amy's Kitchen, BOLD Organic's vegan pizzas, Whole foods etc. Most supermarkets have a Gluten-Free or 'Free From' section in their aisles and freezers.

Green Smoothie

Serves 1

Ingredients

¼ cup water
½ cup pineapple juice
1 ¾ cups green grapes
¼ cup bartlett pear (seeded and halved)
½ cup avocado (pitted, peeled and roughly chopped)
¼ cup broccoli (roughly chopped)
½ cup spinach leaves
Fresh lime juice (to taste)
¼ cup ice cubes

Directions

Place all the ingredients in to a blender and whizz until smooth then pour in to a serving glass

Artichokes and Olive Salad

Serves 3-4

Ingredients
2 cans of chickpeas (drained)
2 cans of artichokes (drained and chopped smaller)
1 cup sundried tomatoes (chopped roughly)
1 cup sliced green olives
1 cup sliced black olives
Handful of rocket leaves
2 green peppers (sliced julienne)
Juice of 2 limes
1 tsp paprika
1 tsp sea salt (or more to taste)

Directions

Add the first 7 ingredients together, mix well. Add the lime juice, paprika and sea salt to taste. Try adding spicy tomato salsa instead of the sundried tomatoes to give the dish more oomph!

Sundried Tomato Hummus

Serves 1-2

Ingredients
1 can of chick peas (drained)
2oz sundried tomatoes (drained)
Juice of half a lemon
2 cloves of garlic (peeled)
1-2 tbsp of filtered water (optional)
Pinch of paprika
Gluten-free bread toasted and cut into horizontal ½ inch
    sticks

Directions

Put the chick peas, sundried tomatoes, juice of lemon,
paprika, garlic in a food processor and pulse until the
mixture is smooth like a hummus, add water if you prefer is
thinner. Now enjoy with some toasted bread, crackers or
with some crudités (carrots, celery, snow peas)

Chili Tofu Stir Fry

Serves 2

Ingredients

1 cup tofu (cut into long strips)
2/3 cup shitake mushrooms (chopped roughly)
1 carrot (peeled, sliced thinly)
1 green pepper (deseeded, julienned)
1 red pepper (deseeded, julienned)
1 tbsp gluten-free soy sauce
½ tsp red chili powder
Salt to taste
2 cloves of garlic (peeled, chopped)
1 tbsp sesame oil

Directions

Fry the tofu a little until brown on all sides lightly and then add the garlic, green peppers, red peppers, carrots and mushrooms stirring on high heat. Add the soy sauce and red chili powder to the stir fry, frying for another 1 minute before serving

Portobello Mushroom Burgers

Serves 1

Ingredients

2 portobello mushrooms (peeled)
Olive oil for brushing and 1tsp for cooking
¼ red pepper (cut in to think strips)
½ white onion (sliced thinly)
1 tsp vegan mayonnaise
½ tsp crushed garlic
Sliced tomato

Directions

1. Brush the mushrooms with some olive oil and bake or grill until they are cooked through about 8 minutes

depending on size - we will use them as our burger buns

2. Sauté the onion and peppers in a little oil while the mushrooms are cooking

3. Mix the mayo and garlic to make a lovely tangy garlic mayo (add some parsley if you like)

4. Assemble the burger using the mushrooms as burger buns and add garlic mayo, tomato, top with the red pepper and onion

5. You could add some vegan cheese to this also if you prefer

Carrot, Orange and Avocado Salad

Serves 4
Ingredients

2 oranges
Zest and juice of 1 orange
3 carrots (halved lengthways and sliced with a veg peeler to
    give thin strips)
Bag of wild rocket
2 avocados (stoned, peeled and sliced)
1 tbsp olive oil

Directions

Segment the two oranges and place in a bowl with the
rocket, carrots and avocado. Mix the orange juice, zest and
oil together with a whisk then toss through the salad to coat

Zucchini Noodles with Tofu and Peppers

Serves 2-3

Ingredients

1 cup tofu (cut into strips)
½ onion (sliced)
1 each of red and yellow bell peppers (julienned)
2 zucchini (courgette - deseeded and sliced thin using a
    mandolin or julienne peeler)
1 pinch paprika
1 red chili (sliced)
½ tsp garlic powder
Salt and pepper to taste
1 tsp olive oil
½ tbsp tomato paste
Fresh Basil, parsley or chives - whatever you have to hand

Directions

Fry the tofu with some olive oil for 2-3 minutes add the red pepper, zucchini, garlic and paprika stirring until the zucchini is cooked through. Add the tomato paste and a drop of water (if needed) sprinkle with fresh herbs, season and serve immediately

Salads

Apple Celery Crunch

Serves 2

Ingredients
2 Green or Red apples (Sliced)
2 Celery sticks (sliced)
1 Green pepper (Medium, sliced julienne)
½ English cucumber (Medium sized, diced)
Couple of handfuls of your favorite greens (romaine or
    iceberg lettuce)
¼ cup of walnut halves
Dressing
Juice of 2 lemons
1-2 tbsp reduced fat coconut milk
2 tbsp olive oil
Sea salt to taste
Freshly ground black pepper to taste

Directions

Mix the olive oil, coconut milk, sea salt, pepper and juice of lemons in a jar put the lid on and give it a good shake to combine. Place all the other ingredients in a large bowl, and pour over the dressing. Easy and fresh!

Tex-Mex Style Quinoa Salad with creamy Avocado Dressing

Serves 4

Ingredients

1 cup uncooked quinoa
1 (15 oz) can black beans (drained and rinsed)
1 small punnet (200g) cherry tomatoes
1 red bell pepper (diced)
1 large avocado (peeled and diced)
½ cup diced cucumber (seeds removed)
½ cup sweet corn (canned or frozen/defrosted)
1 red onion (diced)
Sea Salt and Freshly ground black pepper (to taste)
1 lime, for juicing over the salad
¼ cup chopped cilantro (coriander)

Avocado Dressing

1 ripe avocado (peeled and stone removed)
1 clove garlic (crushed)
¼ cup silken tofu
Water (amount depends on the preferred consistency)
2 tbsp chopped cilantro (fresh coriander)
1 tbsp tahini
1 tbsp chopped spring onion (scallion)
1 tbsp fresh lime juice
¼ tsp ground cumin
1 jalapeno pepper (depending on your taste - use as little or
    as much as you like)
Salt and ground freshly ground black pepper (to taste)

Directions

1. Put 2 cups of water in a medium saucepan, add the quinoa then cover and bring to the boil.
2. Reduce to a low heat and simmer until the water has evaporated and the quinoa is soft and fluffy. This will take 15-20 minutes.
3. Meanwhile to make the Avocado Dressing add all of the dressing ingredients to a food processor or blender and whizz until creamy smooth (adding water to get the consistency you prefer)
4. Combine the quinoa, tomatoes, red bell peppers, black beans, cucumber, avocado, sweetcorn and red onion in a large bowl, stirring with a spoon or use your hands to mix the ingredients well together.
5. Pour the avocado dressing over the salad and stir until all the ingredients are coated. Taste to check seasoning, add if required.
6. Squeeze the fresh lime juice all over the quinoa salad (this prevents the avocado from browning)

7. Sprinkle over the chopped cilantro (coriander) and
   serve immediately or chilled until required.

Balsamic Artichoke Starter

Serves 2-3

Ingredients

2 cans artichoke hearts (drained, quartered)
3 Beets (Peeled, diced)
1 Cup Pomegranate
2 cups Baby spinach
½ cup Balsamic vinegar
2 tbsp Olive oil
Sea salt to taste
Crushed black pepper to taste

Directions

Make the dressing by mixing the oil, balsamic vinegar, salt and pepper in a jar. Combine the rest of the ingredients in a bowl and drizzle the dressing over before serving

Chickpea Salsa Salad

3-4 servings

Ingredients

2 cans of chickpeas (Drained)
1 cup of black olives
2 red onions (Large, thinly sliced)
2 green peppers (Medium sized, diced)
1 red pepper (Medium, diced)
2 tomatoes (Large, diced)
1 tsp red chili powder
½ tsp sea salt
1 tsp crushed black pepper
Juice of 2 lemons
1 tbsp olive oil
2-3 sprigs of fresh basil.

Directions

Combine all ingredients in a bowl and make a dressing mixing the lemon juice, oil salt, pepper and chili powder in a jar until combined. Pour dressing in to the bowl. Top with the basil. Serve with homemade GF brown bread.

Spicy Kidney Bean Salad

Serves 2-3

Ingredients

1 can sweet corn (drained)
1 ½ cups cooked kidney beans
1 jalapeño pepper (chopped)
1 small can pineapple (drained, chopped)
1 green bell pepper (chopped)
Juice of 2 lemons
Salt and pepper to taste
Fresh parsley

Directions

Combine all ingredients in a bowl and pour lemon juice over making sure all the salad is coated in it. Top with fresh parsley

Pomegranate Kale Salad

Serves 2

Ingredients
1 large bunch of kale
¼ cup of pomegranate seeds
¼ cup sliced blanched almonds (toasted)
¼ cup sunflower seeds
1 small granny smith apple (cored, leave peel on)
1 spring onion (chopped)
Dressing
3 tbsp pomegranate juice
2 tbsp red wine vinegar
1 tbsp agave nectar
1 small garlic clove (crushed)
1/4 cup grapeseed oil
Sea salt and freshly ground pepper

Directions

1. Wash the kale and shake off any excess water. Cut away the centre stems and chop the leaves roughly
2. In a large bowl combine the kale with the pomegranate seeds, almonds, sunflowers seeds and spring onions
3. Put all the dressing ingredients together in a bowl and whisk until combined pour a small amount over the salad and toss to coat, add more if required

Caesar Salad

Serves 4 as Main and 6 as starter

Ingredients
1 head romaine (cos) lettuce

Dressing
¼ cup blanched almonds
1 clove garlic (crushed)
¼ cup soy mayonnaise
2 tbsp nutritional yeast
1 tbsp olive oil
2 tbsp lemon juice
1 tbsp capers
1 tbsp dijon mustard
Sea salt & freshly ground black pepper (to taste)

Garlic Croutons

1 Gluten-free baguette or use a gluten-free ciabatta (cut in
    to cubes)
2 cloves garlic (crushed)
2-3 tbsp olive oil

Directions

1. Pre-heat oven to 350F/175C.
2. Toss the cubed bread with the garlic and oil, season
   with sea salt and black pepper and pour on to a
   baking tray
3. Bake for 10 minutes, giving them a stir halfway
   through and keeping an eye so they do not burn.
   Leave to one side to cool
4. Wash and pat dry lettuce with kitchen paper. Tear it
   into smaller pieces and place into a large bowl
5. Whizz all the dressing ingredients in a food
   processor or blender until smooth
6. Add 2-3 tablespoons of water depending on the
   consistency you prefer your dressing to be
7. Add croutons to the bowl before mixing through the
   dressing - make sure all ingredients are evenly
   coated with the dressing and serve immediately

Pad Thai Salad

Serves 3

Ingredients

3 medium zucchinis (courgettes)
3 large carrots
2 spring onions, chopped
1 cup shredded purple cabbage
1 cup cauliflower florets
1 cup mung bean sprouts or radish sprouts (spicy)
    (optional)
½ cup crushed peanuts
½ cup chopped fresh cilantro (coriander) – optional

Sauce

¼ cup tahini
¼ cup almond butter (or cashew butter)
¼ cup tamari (gluten-free, as required)
2 tbsp agave
2 tbsp lime juice
1 clove garlic, crushed
1 tsp fresh root ginger, peeled and grated

Directions

1. Using a julienne peeler (or a mandolin / spiralizer) make noodles from the carrots and zucchinis and place in a bowl with the shredded cabbage, spring onions, cauliflower, bean sprouts, peanuts and cilantro (if using)
2. Mix all the ingredients for the sauce together in a bowl with a whisk. It will be thick, this is fine
3. Pour the sauce over the vegetables and toss to ensure they are coated evenly then serve

Pear and Walnut Salad

Serves 2

Ingredients
2 cups (2 large handfuls) leafy greens
2 green pears (diced or sliced)
½ cup / 60g walnuts (rough chopped)
2-3 tbsp balsamic vinegar
1 tbsp olive oil
1 tbsp Dijon mustard
Salt and black pepper to taste

Directions

Combine salad leaves, pear and walnuts in a bowl. Put the balsamic, Dijon, oil, salt and pepper in a jar and shake vigorously to combine. Pour as much or as little dressing as you like over the salad and mix well. This makes for a tasty and gourmet salad

Lunch

Red Lentil Soup

Serves 2-3

Ingredients

1 cup red lentils (washed)
4 cups / 1ltr water or veg stock/broth
1 tsp chili powder
1 onion (diced)
½ tsp turmeric powder
½ tsp all spice powder
2-3 garlic cloves (peeled, chopped thinly)
2 tbsp olive oil
Chopped cilantro (coriander)

Directions

1. In a medium sized pot heat the oil and add the onion and garlic, cook on a low heat for 5 minutes before adding the spices and lentils
2. Stir then add the stock/water, cover and cook on medium for 15 minutes or until the lentils are cooked - red lentils don't take long to cook and are a good choice for light vegan gluten-free lunch
3. You can whizz the soup up with a hand blender or in a food processor or leave it chunky, I like to blend up about 2 cups and add back so it's the best of both! Top it with some dried chili seeds (if you like it hot!) and some fresh herbs like cilantro, basil or parsley

Chickpea Burgers with Tomato Salsa

Makes 6-8 burgers

Ingredients
1 x 19oz can chickpeas (drained and rinsed)
2 cups cooked brown rice
3-4 green onions (sliced finely)
¼ cup fresh cilantro (finely chopped)
2 cloves garlic (crushed)
3 tbsp grated fresh ginger
3 tbsps lemon juice
2 tsp curry powder
2 tsp cumin
2 tsp ground coriander
2 tsp garam masala
1 tsp red chili flakes
1 tsp sea salt
2 flax eggs
1 tbsp gram flour or chana (chickpea) flour
Coconut / vegetable oil, for frying

Salsa
3 plum tomatoes (chopped)
1 onion (diced)
2 tbsp olive oil
½ tsp fresh lime juice
½ tsp chili flakes or fresh
Sea Salt
Freshly ground black pepper

Directions

1. To make the salsa add all the ingredients together and let them marinade while you make the burgers
2. Place 1 cup of brown rice and ¾ of the can of chickpeas in a processor and pulse a few times until combined but not pureed together
3. Add the remaining chickpeas a few at a time and pulse, we want them combined in some to be left whole
4. Pour the mixture in to a bowl, add the remainder of the rice and the rest of the ingredients and mix well so everything is combined. Form burgers from the mixture (around 6-8 burgers)
5. Heat a frying pan or skillet over a high heat and add the oil. Add the patties and fry on each side until golden and crisp, this should take around 5 minutes per side
6. Serve with the salsa

Chili Non Carne

Serves 2-3

Ingredients

1 cup black eyed peas (boiled until cooked through)
1 can white (haricot) beans
2 tomatoes (large, diced small)
1 zucchini (diced small)
1 carrot (medium, diced small)
2 onions (large, diced small)
2 jalapeño peppers (chopped small)
2 green or red peppers (deseeded, diced)
½ tsp red chili powder (add more if you like a hotter chili)
½ tsp all spice powder
½ tsp coriander powder
Salt to taste
Black pepper to taste
2-3 garlic cloves (peeled, crushed)
1 can of chopped tomatoes
1 tbsp tomato paste
1 ripe avocado (diced)
2 tbsp olive oil
Vegetable Stock (optional)

Directions

1. Heat olive oil in a medium sized pot. Add the onions, green peppers, carrots, and tomatoes to it. Cook them until the carrots are slightly soft before adding the black eyed peas and stir for a while on high heat

2. After 3-4 minutes add all the seasonings and the garlic, ginger and the jalapeño peppers. Stir for another 4 minutes on medium heat then add the can of chopped tomatoes, tomato paste and some vegetable broth (if needed) cook on a simmer for 10 minutes. Add the white beans and simmer for a further 5 minutes
3. Top with chopped avocado and serve with cauliflower rice and a wedge of lime

Green Gazpacho

Serves 4

Ingredients

1 English cucumber
1 yellow bell pepper
¼ small sweet white onion
1 ripe avocado
1 cup vegetable stock
1 tsp freshly squeezed lime juice
2 tbsp extra virgin olive oil
¾ cup fresh cilantro (coriander)
1 clove garlic (crushed)
1 Thai chili
1 tsp sea salt
Basil leaves (to garnish)

Directions

1. Cut a two inch piece off the cucumber and put to one side – this is to garnish at the end
2. Chop all the ingredients roughly (apart from the basil leaves and tomatoes) and add to a blender - whizz until smooth then pass through a sieve sing a spoon to make sure you get all the liquid, discard the solids that are left
3. You can now refrigerate the soup for a few hours if you have the time. If not serve straight away in glasses. Chop the reserved cucumber finely and add to the top of the soup with chopped basil leaves and sprinkle over some paprika

Parsnip Chowder

Serves 6

Ingredients

1 ½ tablespoons olive oil

1 large white onion (chopped)

4 medium potatoes (peeled and finely diced)

1 pound parsnips (peeled and cut in to large dice)

4 cups water with 2 vegetable bouillon cubes (make sure
    they are vegan and GF)

1 tbsp all-purpose seasoning blend (Like Mrs. Dash) Or use
    mixed herbs

2 cups rice milk (use soy or almond if you prefer)

¼ cup fresh parsley (finely chopped)

1 - 2 tbsp fresh dill (finely chopped)

Freshly ground black pepper to taste

Directions

1. Heat the oil in a large pot and add the onion. Cook
    over a medium heat until it browns then add the
    potatoes, parsnips, vegetable stock and seasoning
    blend.
2. Bring to the boil then turn to a low heat, cover and
    simmer until the parsnips and potatoes are soft. This
    should take about 20 minutes.
3. Remove two cupfuls of potatoes and parsnips with a
    large slotted spoon to a pasta bowl. Mash well
    before stirring them back through the chowder.
4. Add the rice milk, parsley, and dill. Season to taste
    with black pepper. Heat it back up and serve
    immediately with some more dill for garnish

Mushroom and Pine Nuts Rice Stuffed Peppers

Serves 4

Ingredients

4 green/red peppers (tops and seeds removed)
1 cup Shitake mushrooms (or any other)
½ cup veggie broth
1 ½ cups wild rice (cooked, drained)
½ cup pine nuts
1 tsp salt
¼ tsp turmeric powder
¼ tsp all spice powder
2 cloves garlic (peeled, chopped)
2-4 tbsp olive oil

Directions

1. Preheat the oven to 375f / 180c degrees
2. Heat a skillet with olive oil and add the garlic, stirring until you can smell the garlic but make sure you don't burn it as it will go bitter
3. Add the mushrooms, pine nuts, spices and seasoning. Stir until pine nuts go slightly brown and then add the broth
4. Add the rice stirring minimally to make sure you don't break the rice until the liquid is absorbed
5. Grease the baking tray lightly and stuff hollowed out peppers with the rice mixture to the top
6. Place the stuffed peppers on the baking tray and bake for 15-20minutes

Curried Pumpkin Bisque

Serves 4

Ingredients

1 (15-ounce) can pumpkin puree
1 tsp light brown sugar
1 tbsp curry powder
1 (15-ounce) can unsweetened coconut milk
1 cup vegetable broth (canned or made with a bouillon
    cube)
Salt and freshly ground black pepper
2 tbsp pumpkin seeds (optional - to garnish before serving)

Directions

1. Place the pumpkin puree, curry powder and brown sugar in to a pot over a medium heat
2. Add the coconut milk a little at a time whisking until smooth
3. Add the vegetable stock until you achieve your desired thickness (you might not need the full cup)
4. Season with salt and freshly ground black pepper
5. Simmer for 10 minutes stirring occasionally. Taste and add more seasonings if required. Serve hot and garnish with the pumpkin seeds if using

Eggplant Ragout

Serves 6

Ingredients

2 eggplants / aubergines (large, with seeds scooped out, diced)
1 red onion (large, diced)
1 can tomatoes (drained, chopped)
1 can chickpeas (drained)
2 green peppers (deseeded and diced)
1 butternut squash (small, deseeded and diced)
½ tbsp tomato paste
4 garlic gloves (chopped)
1 tsp red chili powder
1 tsp turmeric powder
1 tsp salt
Pepper to taste
3 tbsp olive oil
4-5 sprigs of basil

Directions

1. In a medium sized pot heat olive oil and add the onion, stir until slightly sautéed, add the garlic and cook lightly but take care you don't burn it
2. Now add the tomatoes, eggplant, chickpeas, green pepper, squash, chili powder, salt, turmeric powder and tomato paste
3. Cover and cook on low heat until the eggplant is cooked but not mushy
4. Serve topped with a sprig of basil and a little all spice powder

Cauliflower Pizza Bites

Makes: 24 Bites

Ingredients
2 cups of grated cauliflower (approx one medium head)
1 tsp oregano
2 tsp parsley
¼ tsp garlic powder
2 tbsp coconut oil
1-2 tbsp Frank's Hot Sauce
1 flax egg (1 tbsp ground flaxseed / linseed and 3 tbsp
    warm water)
½ cup firm tofu
½ cup chickpeas (cooked and drained)

Directions

1. Pre-heat your oven to 450F / 230C and spray a mini muffin tray with some healthy oil
2. Mix the flaxseed with warm water and leave to one side to 'thicken'
3. Stir-fry the grated cauliflower in a little oil over a hot heat for 5 minutes until its translucent then put in to a bowl
4. Blend the remaining ingredients in a food processor then add to the cauliflower and mix well to combine
5. Place spoonfuls of the mixture in to the muffin moulds, pressing the mixture down gently so it sticks together while cooking
6. Cook for 20-25 minutes or until golden, remove from the oven and allow to cool slightly while still in the pan – do not remove while still hot as they will break up!

7. Serve with your favorite organic or natural pizza
   sauce

Veggie Quesadillas

Serves 2

Ingredients

2 large gluten-free tortillas
1 cup hummus (use the sundried tomato recipe from page
    11 or store-bought)

Filling

¼ cup onion (chopped)
2 cups of mixed vegetables - I love red bell pepper,
    mushrooms and broccoli
½ tsp cumin powder

½ tsp chili powder
1 tbsp olive oil
Vegetable stock (optional)
Vegan Cheddar (optional)

Guacamole
1 medium avocado (make sure it's ripe)
2 Tbsp chopped cilantro (coriander)
2 Tbsp finely chopped scallions (spring onions) or red
    onions
2 Tbsp chopped tomatoes (or more to taste)
1 tsp fresh lime juice, plus more to taste
1 green jalapeno (more or less to taste)
1 garlic clove (crushed)

Directions

1. Heat a large nonstick pan on medium, add the olive oil. When hot add the chopped onions, cook for 3-4 minutes until softened and translucent
2. Add a little vegetable stock if the onions start sticking to the pan
3. Add the rest of the chopped vegetables, cook for 2-3 min until they are cooked
4. Stir in cumin and chili powder and put to one side.
5. Place a tortilla on plate / chopping board and spread one half of it half the hummus. Top the other half with the stir-fried veggies and cheddar if using
6. Fold the hummus part over on top of the veggies and press down lightly
7. Griddle the wraps over a medium heat for 2-3 min per side, make sure you don't burn. You can use a panini machine either

8. Peel the avocado and remove the stone, mash with a fork or pulse in a food processor. Stir in the cilantro, scallions, and lime juice then mash or pulse again. Add the chopped tomatoes and serve in ramekins with the quesadillas

Tomato Spaghetti

Serves 4

Ingredients

2 cups / 250-300g any kind of mushrooms
4 cloves of garlic
1 red pepper (deseeded, julienned)
1 cup / 200g tofu (diced, browned on all sides a little)
4 large tomatoes (diced)
4 zucchini (use the mandolin / julienne peeler to make into
   spaghetti)
½ cup / 125ml vegetable stock
2 tbsp olive oil
1 tsp paprika powder
2 tbsp oregano

Directions

1. Heat a large skillet with olive oil and add the
   mushrooms, red pepper, garlic, and cook until any
   liquid has dried up
2. Now add the oregano, paprika powder, salt and
   pepper to taste then add the tomatoes and zucchini.
   Let the mixture simmer for 15-20 minutes adding tofu
   at the end

Dinner

Pizza with Cauliflower Crust

Makes 2 small or one large pizza

Ingredients
Crust
3 cups cauliflower (ground, should look like rice)
5 flax 'eggs' (see introduction)
1 ¼ cup almond flour
1 tsp sea salt
1 tsp garlic powder

Tomato sauce
4 tomatoes (boiled, peeled) or 1 can of chopped tomatoes
1 tsp oregano

1 tbsp tomato paste
Salt and pepper to taste
4 garlic cloves (crushed)

Toppings (use whatever you like, below is just a
 suggestion)
1 red pepper (medium, julienne)
1 red onion (sliced thin)
1 packaged tempeh (crumbled)
4 button mushrooms (sliced)

Directions

1. Mix the flax eggs and leave in the fridge for use later
2. Pre-heat your oven to 450 degrees and line your baking tray with parchment paper
3. Mix all the ingredients for the crust in a large bowl and combine until a thick, dough forms
4. Take 1 cup of the mixture and roll out your pizza crusts on the baking tray using grease proof paper on top so it doesn't stick to the rolling pin, spread it out into a circle of uniform thickness
5. Bake the pizza crusts without the toppings for 20 minutes until they are browned slightly
6. Take the ingredients for the tomato sauce and blend them in a blender - taste for seasoning
7. Add the toppings after spreading on the tomato sauce and put the pizza back in the oven for another 10 minutes until golden

Coconut Curry with Rice

Serves 6

Ingredients
1 red onion (large, diced)
1 broccoli head (medium, florets broken)
2 cups of green beans (chopped small)
2 cans of tomatoes (diced)
1 can coconut milk
4 cloves garlic (peeled, crushed)
1 tbsp ginger (peeled, crushed)
1 tsp turmeric powder
2 tsp coriander powder
1 tsp all spice powder
2 tbsp coconut oil

Directions

1. Heat a large pot with some coconut oil in it. Add the onion, ginger and garlic
2. Cook until the onion has softened. Add the spices to the onion and cook them until they are fragrant
3. Now add the tomatoes, green beans, broccoli and coconut milk. Leave the heat on medium until the mixture comes to a boil
4. Then reduce the heat and cover the pot letting everything simmer for 10-15 minutes
5. Uncover the pot and cook for a further 5 minutes until the sauce has thickened up a bit
6. Serve with normal boiled white rice, mushroom rice or cauliflower rice

Eggplant Parmigiana

Serves 6

Ingredients

2 medium eggplants (aubergines)
Sea salt
½ cup sweet vidalia onion vinaigrette
2 tbsp water
1 cup fine dry gluten-free bread crumbs
1 tsp Italian seasoning
½ teaspoon garlic powder
Freshly ground black pepper
Olive oil, for drizzling
2 cups prepared marinara sauce (heated)
1 cup Daiya mozzarella shreds (or any other vegan cheese
    you prefer)

Directions

1. Pre-heat oven to 375F / 190C and line a baking sheet with parchment paper
2. Prick the eggplants all over with a fork and place on a microwaveable dish and cook in the microwave for 3-4 minutes until soft but still firm
3. When they are cool enough to handle slice the eggplants in to ½ inch slices
4. Pour the vinaigrette and water in to a bowl. Place the gluten-free breadcrumbs, Italian seasoning, garlic powder and black pepper in to a separate bowl. Mix well to combine, then dip each eggplant slice in to liquid before dipping in the breadcrumb mixture. Make sure all the slices are coated evenly
5. Place the slices on to the baking sheet and bake in the oven for 15 minutes or until golden
6. Heat the marinara sauce and preheat the broiler (grill) once they slices are cooked place them in a baking dish, top with the sauce and sprinkle over the cheese then place under the broiler until golden and bubbling

Mushroom Stroganoff

Serves 4

Ingredients

12 ounces of large portobello mushrooms (stems removed,
    cut into large chunks)
4 ounces shitake mushrooms (halved)
3 tbsp olive oil
Sea salt and freshly ground black pepper
1 medium onion (chopped)
3 gloves garlic (crushed)
2 tbsp gluten-free soy sauce
2 tbsp sherry, cognac or dry vermouth (all optional)
½ cup vegetable broth / stock
1 cup frozen baby onions (thawed)
1 cup vegan sour cream
2 tbsp flat leaf Italian parsley (chopped)

Directions

1. Heat two tablespoons of oil in a frying pan until really hot then add the mushrooms and cook for 5 minutes until the liquid has evaporated then remove from the pan and set aside
2. Heat the remaining oil in the pan and add the chopped onion, saute for 5 minutes until they have softened then add the garlic. Season with salt and pepper to taste and add the mushrooms back to the pan along with any juices that have come out of them
3. Add the soy sauce and alcohol to the pan and cook until it has completely evaporated then add the vegetable stock and baby onions
4. Cook for 3 – 4 minutes until the stock has reduced by half and the onions have warmed through. Reduce the heat to low and pour in the sour cream, stir gently until heated through. Serve over steamed rice, rice noodles or gluten-free pasta - sprinkle the parsley over just before serving

Creamy Avocado Carbonara

Serves 2-3

Ingredients

3 tbsp extra virgin olive oil
2 medium zucchinis (courgettes) - julienned
¼ cup water
1 medium sized ripe Avocado, pitted
Juice and zest of half a lemon
3 garlic cloves, crushed
Pinch of sea salt (to taste)
¼ cup of fresh parley
1/3 cup of walnuts, chopped and toasted
Freshly ground pepper (to taste)
Fresh parsley, to garnish

Directions

1. Heat one tablespoon of olive oil in a pan and add the zucchini and cook over a medium heat for one minute then add the water and cook until soft, about 6 minutes
2. While the zucchini is cooking make the sauce by add the lemon juice, garlic and remaining olive oil to a blender and whizz until smooth
3. Add the avocado ¼ cup of parsley and seasoning then whizz again until the mixture is creamy and smooth
4. Put the zucchini in to a bowl and pour over the sauce and toss to coat. To serve top with the chopped walnuts, parsley and lemon zest and season to your taste

Cauliflower Tacos

Makes 8 wraps / tacos so serves 4-8 people

Ingredients
Roasted Cauliflower
1 medium head cauliflower broke in to florets)
2 tbsp olive oil
½ tsp sea salt

Spiced Chick Peas
1 15-ounce can chick peas (rinsed and drained)
1 tbsp olive oil
½ tsp sea salt
¼ tsp cayenne pepper or chili powder (to taste, add more if
    you prefer them hotter)
¼ tsp dried oregano
¼ tsp ground cumin

To Serve

8 tbsp of your favorite Vegan Pesto (I love basil and pine nut pesto with this)

8 gluten-free tortilla wraps or corn tacos

Avocado, chopped tomatoes and lettuce

Tofutti Sour Cream (or any other vegan sour cream - optional)

Directions

1. Preheat oven to 425F / 210C
2. Put the cauliflower florets in large bowl and drizzle over the oil and season with the sea salt. Pour on to a baking tray and cook for 15 minutes, take out and stir and put back in the oven for 5-10 minutes until brown and tender
3. Meanwhile, mix all the spicy chick pea ingredients together. Spread on to a baking sheet and bake for 10 to 15 minutes. Check if they are crispy, if not bake for a further 10 minutes
4. Heat the tortillas through according to packet instructions
5. Spread each tortilla with one tablespoon of pesto. Place half a cup of cauliflower and a tablespoon of spicy chick peas on top of the pesto.
6. Add avocado, tomatoes and lettuce if using. Garnish with fresh cilantro (coriander). Serve with remaining chickpeas and some tossed salad

Crispy Tofu Goujons

Serves 1-2

Ingredients

½ a block of tofu (pressed and sliced in to thick gougons)
¼ cup unsweetened almond milk or non-dairy milk of choice
½ tbsp Dijon mustard
¼ cup almond flour
2 tbsp unsweetened flaked coconut
2 tbsp black sesame seeds
Pinch sea salt
Freshly ground black pepper
¼ tsp paprika

Directions

1. Pre-heat oven to 350F / 180C
2. Place the mustard and milk in to a bowl. In a second bowl mix the almond flour, coconut and sesame seeds
3. Dip each goujon in to the milk mixture then in to the almond mixture ensuring they are coated evenly
4. Place parchment paper on to a baking sheet and add the coated goujons
5. Bake for 20 minutes turning half way through
6. Serve with sweet potato fries and coleslaw (see snacks and sides for recipes)

Lasagna

Serves 3-4

Ingredients
1 can sweet corn (small drained)
1 can red kidney beans
2 eggplant / aubergine (deseeded and diced)
2 cups Daiya cheddar or mozzarella cheese (grated, or
    sliced)
¾ cup black olives
½ cupl vegetable stock
2 cups of mushrooms
1 whole cabbage (carefully peel off leaves and keep aside)

2 cans chopped tomatoes
4 garlic cloves
3-4 tbsp olive oil
Few sprigs of fresh basil
Homemade pesto to serve (optional)

Directions

1. Preheat your oven to 375F / 190C
2. Heat a skillet with 2 tbsp olive oil and add the garlic
3. Add the eggplant and mushrooms – stir fry until the mushrooms are dry
4. Add the chopped tomatoes and stock, stir for a while until the tomatoes have cooked down then leave to simmer until the eggplant is cooked now add the kidney beans and simmer for a few minutes
5. Have a Pyrex or any other baking dish ready greased with some olive oil and start layering the lasagna
6. Take the cabbage leaves and use them as pasta sheets to cover the baking dish. Spoon over the eggplant mixture and sprinkle a handful of sweet corn and olives over it
7. Cover with a layer of cabbage leaves and sprinkle daiya mozzarella (or any other dairy free cheese) over it. Then layer the mixture again and repeat the last step until the dish is filled to the top
8. Top with a generous layer of cheese and then put it in the oven for 20 minutes
9. Let the lasagna rest for 15 minutes before cutting and drizzle with homemade pesto and garnish with fresh basil before serving

Veggie Fried Rice

Serves 2-3

Ingredients

1 yellow onion
½ cup frozen peas
1 large carrot (diced)
½ red bell pepper (diced)
1 cup chanterelle mushrooms (sliced)
½ cup vegetarian broth
1½ cups rice
1 tbsp olive oil
2 garlic cloves (crushed)
Salt and pepper to taste

Directions

1. Boil the rice and cook it until done. Leave aside to cool

2. In a large skillet heat olive oil and add the onion and mushroom sautéing until the water from mushrooms has cooked off
3. Add the garlic, red pepper and carrots cooking on low heat until the carrots are cooked
4. Now add the broth and peas and slowly incorporate the cooled rice, stirring with a large spatula making sure you don't break the rice
5. Serve it once all the broth has absorbed and peas are cooked

Singapore Fried Noodles

Serves 2

Ingredients
2 tbsp grapeseed oil
1 inch piece of ginger (peeled and grated finely)
4 cloves garlic (crushed)
½ onion, sliced
½ red bell pepper (cut into thin strips)
½ green bell pepper (cut into thin strips)
1 carrot (peeled and cut into thin strips)
1 stalk celery (sliced at an angle)
½ cup bean sprouts
5 broccoli florets (cut in half)
1 x 8 oz pack vermicelli rice noodles
2 tbsp yellow curry powder
¼ tsp red chili flakes
1 tbsp gluten-free soy sauce (or tamari)
½ cup coconut milk

Directions

1. Remove the rice noodles from the packet and prepare according to the instructions
2. In a large frying pan heat the oil over a high heat then add the garlic, onions and ginger and sauté for 1 minute
3. Add the rest of the vegetables and cook for 5 minutes until the onion has started to soften
4. Next add the rice noodles, chili flakes, curry powder, soy sauce and coconut milk. Using a tongs toss everything together to coat in the sauce and serve immediately

Aloo Gobi - Cauliflower and Potato

Serves 4

Ingredients
2 tbsp vegetable oil
1 large onion (large dice)
½ head cauliflower (broke in to small florets)
2 medium potatoes (peeled and cut in to large dice)
1 tsp ground turmeric
¼ tsp chili powder / cayenne
½ tsp sea salt
1 tbsp water
2 cans chopped tomatoes
½ tsp cumin seeds
½ tsp mustard seeds
3 cloves of garlic (crushed)
1 thumb-sized piece of ginger, about 1-inch long (finely
    crushed)
1 bunch fresh coriander finely chopped

Directions

1. Heat your oil in a large saucepan / skillet that has a
   lid
2. Add the onion, cumin seeds and mustard seeds and
   cook on a low heat until the onions are translucent
3. Add the garlic, ginger, turmeric and chili powder -
   mix well and do not let the garlic burn
4. Add the canned tomatoes and a pinch of salt
5. Now add the cauliflower and potatoes, add some veg
   stock or water if needed. Stir the cauliflower and
   potatoes to ensure they are all covered in the sauce

6. Place the lid on the pan and simmer on a low-medium heat for 20 minutes
7. Sprinkle with coriander and serve. Poppadum's are perfect with this! (make sure they are the traditional ones which are made from lentil flour)

Bonus Recipes
A little longer than 30 minutes but worth it

Potato and Tomato Bake

Serves 4

Ingredients
4 large potatoes (peeled)
2 large tomatoes (sliced)
1 onion (sliced)
1 ¼ cup soy milk
4 tsp gluten-free corn flour
Tepid water
½ tsp sea salt
Few sprigs of fresh thyme (or any other herbs you prefer)
½ cup grated vegan cheddar (or your favorite vegan
    cheese)
Olive oil
1 tsp black pepper (or to taste)

2 tsp garlic powder

Directions

1. Place the potatoes in a pan of boiling water and cook for 7-10 minutes until half cooked. Take them out and slice with a knife carefully as they are hot
2. Brush a baking / Pyrex dish with olive oil and start layering starting with the potatoes then onion and season each layer as you go with the garlic, salt, pepper and herbs
3. To make your sauce in a small bowl mix the corn flour with tepid water until is like a paste. Heat the soy milk in a saucepan and when hot but not boiling add the corn flour mixture whisking all the time. Cook for 1 minute stirring continuously. It should have a thick-ish consistency
4. Pour this over the potatoes and cook in the oven for 25 minutes, take out and top with the tomatoes and cheese. Put back in the oven for 10-15 minutes. Serve with a rocket or spinach salad. This is also delicious served cold as a side dish at barbeques

Veggie Shepherd Pie

Serves 4

Ingredients
Filling
1-2 tbsps extra virgin olive oil
4 cloves of garlic, crushed
1 butternut squash (peeled and diced)
1 zucchini (courgette) (diced)
1 can of tomatoes
1 tbsp balsamic vinegar
1 cup vegetable broth / stock
3 carrots (medium, peeled and diced)
1 large onion (diced)
1 small head of cauliflower broken in to small florets
1 tbsp of tomato paste
1 cup vegetable stock / broth
Gluten-free Worcestershire sauce (Lea and Perrins)
Sea salt and freshly ground pepper
Few sprigs of fresh thyme

Mash
4 large potatoes (peeled and cut in to large chunks)
Olive oil (you can use a vegan butter if you prefer)
1 tsp Dijon mustard
Sea salt & pepper to taste
Fresh herbs – I like parsley and chives

Directions

1. Preheat your grill to hot or oven to 350f / 180c
2. Place the potatoes in a large saucepan and cover with cold water. Cook until they are tender, this

should take about 15-20 minutes depending on the size of your chunks. Mash with some olive oil, Dijon mustard, sea salt and pepper to taste

3. While your potatoes are cooking heat some oil in a skillet and add the onions. After a few minutes add the rest of the veggies and the garlic

4. Add the can of tomatoes, tomato paste and broth / stock and a good few splashes of Worcestershire sauce. Add the thyme sprigs and let it all simmer for 10 minutes and until the sauce has thickened a bit. Taste for seasoning and add sea salt and pepper (if needed)

5. Place the filling in an oven proof dish and then add the mash on top. I like to line the top roughly with a fork and make a peak in the centre

6. This will cook in 10-15 minutes under a hot grill or if you have a little bit of extra time bake it in the oven for 35-40 minutes. I like to serve some petit pois on the side

7.

Snacks & Sides

1. Fruit salad - Make a fresh fruit salad using apples, pomegranate, bananas, kiwis and pears. Drizzle with lemon juice or soy yogurt before enjoying or you can also use any seasonal fruits that you like. Mango, passion fruit, and papaya make a wonderful combination.
2. Kale chips - Make kale chips by washing and drying the kale leave, bake them in the oven at 375 degrees sprinkled with your choice of seasoning until they are crisp.
3. Granola bars - Make your own gluten-free vegan granola bar by toasting seeds and nuts you like and drizzling them with honey and layering flat on a baking sheet. Bake for 15 minutes.
4. Try almond or cashew butter with apple. This makes for a great, healthy and filling snack.
5. Salsa and corn chips – make your own salsa by blending together chopped tomatoes, jalapeño peppers, some pineapple and red bell pepper. Enjoy with some corn chips, top with dairy free cheese and bake for 10 minutes in a hot oven.

6. Smoothies – Enjoy coconut or almond milk smoothies with seasonal fruits and throw in a little ginger and mint for stronger taste.

Sides

1. Coleslaw – Make coleslaw with red and white cabbage, carrots, red onions and a dressing made of vegan mayonnaise.
2. Roast some thinly sliced sweet potato sprinkled with sea salt and pepper and olive oil, they make a great alternative to French fries.
3. Makes some garlic and turmeric rice by frying some garlic cloves with turmeric and olive oil and cooking the rice in vegetable broth.
4. Make some potato mash with coconut milk and nut butter. Sweet potato mash tastes even better this way.
5. Roast some leeks and carrots with crushed garlic cloves and some vegan seasoning in the oven as a side to a soup.
6. Make some fresh guacamole with ripe avocados, onions, tomatoes and jalapeno peppers as a side to a Mexican dish or just to enjoy with any dish.

Conclusion

Being on a vegan and gluten-free diet does not mean you have to be restricted in your kitchen. This book gives you many flavourful recipe ideas that can be whipped up quickly and also taste wonderful. Experimenting with vegan and gluten-free ingredients gives you a new perspective on the way you eat and also broadens your food horizons. So, don't be limited because of your diet. Be brave, and try different combination of the various gluten-free, vegan substitutes available.

The combination of ingredients used in this book is not an exact science. You can try other combinations with the same recipes and adapt them to your taste. The best way to go about trying new recipes is to learn as much as you can about your ingredients. Learn to read food labels and make sure the ingredients you buy are both vegan and gluten-free. Conquering this diet should be no problem if give the above recipes a try. Everything is fresh and full of the nutrition your body needs. The main concern with vegan diets that are also gluten-free has always been about whether this diet fulfills the nutritional needs of human beings. Apart from organic products, fortified approved grain based cereals that are fortified with Vitamins can also help fulfill your nutritional needs if you're worried about changing over to this diet.

Many of the ingredients listed are also high energy giving vitamins and proteins. You are guaranteed not to feel famished after such meals. So, venture out into your grocery store and find out what gluten-free vegan ingredients you can find for your shelf and start your new journey towards a healthier and vibrant new you.

Experiment, get out of your comfort zone and most of all enjoy it!

About the Author

Best-selling Author Sophie Miller is a long-time lover of food and cooking. Her first memory of cooking is making Bolognese with her mother, and scones and brown bread with her grandmother. She has worked as a chef in numerous restaurants and ran her own café which concentrated on healthy eating. She loves going to farmers markets with her produce and sharing stories and recipes with other stall owners. She has ten publications to her name so far and is currently working on more exciting cookbooks.

Sophie eats a mostly wheat-free diet, the bloated stomach was not a good look for her! She loves veggies from her own vegetable patch and she really enjoys to cook and bake vegan goods for her best friend. Her husband eats everything (apart from cucumber) so she cooks a range of different food to keep the entire household happy.

Sophie lives in the country with her husband, six dogs, two horses, 11 ducks and 4 chickens! Friends call her the most organised person they know and love going to dinner parties in her house. Christmas dinner is traditionally ALWAYS in Sophie's abode and family travel from far and wide to celebrate the day there, enjoying a spectacular five course meal... She loves travelling and experimenting with dishes she has tasted while abroad when she gets back.

Grab one of her Sophie's other books below, you won't be disappointed....

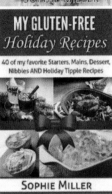